THE INTERVIEW - THAT CHANGED MY LIFE

DHANESH GHANASHYAM GAWDE

Contents

Contents

FOREWORD

<u>Name of the Author:</u> - Dhanesh Ghanashyam Gawde

He is Dhanesh Ghanashyam Gawde, a 21 years boy. He belongs from Goa. He has recently pursued with his BBI(Banking and Insurance) Graduation from Shri Pancham Khemraj College from Sawantwadi, Maharashtra. He has also completed with his Diploma of Computer Engineering. His hobbies are: - Listening to music, Cooking, Gardening, Writing and Reading. His aim is to be a successful Writer and an Author. He loves to write shayaris, quotes, poems. He has also published his 8 solo books on Amazon, Flipkart, Google and Notion Press.

His some books are as follows: -

1. 50 Reasons to live your life
2. Dil se Judi 50 Shaayaris
3. To stay or to leave: - Forgiving the unforgivable
4. (Same book as above but in marathi edition)
5. Mobile addiction in today's youth
6. (Same book as above but in Marathi edition)
7. 50 All time great shaayaris
8. The Devil Doll

You can even follow him on his Instagram handle. His instagram id is mentioned below.

Insta id: - unreliableuniform62

Thank you.

Preface

This is a story of a girl named Yamini who has suffered a lot since her childhood. She has fought a lot in her life.

Will she able to fight in the future too?

Read to Know.

I

THE DREAM JOB

I cannot believe! My dream came true! I am selected for professional photography. I ... I am literally crying! Since my angelic mom and dad passed away, this is the first time I have heard something good. Finally, after 8 years, I will not have to work as a server in that shabby restaurant.

Mom and dad, I hope you will be proud of your little Yami.

I cannot wait to go to the studio tomorrow.

I woke up at 5 AM the next day itself. I was so excited! I get in my small-mini car and ride to the studio. Finally! I am so nervous about how my work will go. I will try my best!

"Good morning, you must be Yamini."

I hear a voice from the back.

"Welcome to your first day at photography. I am Yash. Hope you do well."

"Oh! Good morning Mr. Yash". I reply with a pleasant voice.

"Nice to meet you too, you can call me just Yash, he replied with a smile on his face that was actually a smirk.

"You must proceed to your room. We have arranged it for you." Said yash.

"My own room". I was shocked. I have never been treated so well in my life!

"By the way I am also a part-time employee. So no need to feel alone." He said again.

"Thank you, yash", I responded and went to see my room.

Beautiful! That was the only thought that came to my mind after seeing my room. It was mind blowing. Everything was perfect. Now the only thing that was left for me was to meet the director and start getting used to my dream job.

…………..

OH! I am tired. The director asked me to click many photos and now my hand hurts. However, the good news is that he was impressed by my work! Now I can finally live in peace with no stress. I wish mom and dad were here.

I wish they could see me... I wish...

II
SOMEONE NEW

Oh! I want to sleep. This freaking alarm! Ohm! Shut the heck up. Oh, shit! It is 08:40AM. Have to reach to the studio until nine. What the fu…!

Yamini hurry up!

Hurry up yamini or you are going to have a bad day today!

I sit in my car and drive at almost a full speed. I know that is illegal but I cannot help!

Thank goodness! I reached on time!

Ouch! "Are you fucking stupid! You fool!

I heard this when I was laying on the ground. I bumped into someone. Of course! Thanks to my clumsy ass.

"And you are still listening you idiot". I again heard someone cussing me. It was a woman of my age. In fact a pretty woman but with full confidence.

"I am sorry. I was in a hurry, I apologized."

"Sorry? Are you blind? You just…

When she was about to say more, someone interrupted her.

"It's ok Gauri. Stop cussing her! Said yash.

"You just shut your mouth you chameleon!" gauri replied.

"I have told you how many times not to call me that, said yash.

It was as if two asteroids were about to collide.

"Okay guys! Stop fighting like kids." I tried to calm them down.

"Another thing, can I ask your name miss BTW, I am Gauri." She said.

"She is Yamini" before I could answer, yash already responded with a quick tongue.

"Nobody asked you, you lizard!"

Ugh! Not again, why are they arguing? I thought and was confused too. I did not want to ruin my day. Therefore, I let them fight and went to my room to learn about some photography tricks.

It had been much time since I was working, so I peeped out of my room and guess what!

Gauri and yash, they were still fighting like freaking dinosaurs.

I had to stop them. However, how? Therefore, I shouted aloud, "Stop fighting you two idiots!" they both looked at me with a confused look. Yash was done with arguing, so he went back to work. Now, there were just two of us, gauri and me.

"He is such a jerk! Isn't he?" gauri asked me while coming towards me. She really reacted like nothing happen between the two of them. While I was thinking of this, she relented in between and insisted me to forget of all the dispute happened between us.

"I am a little stupid you know. I cannot control my tongue when I speak. I hope you don't take it seriously."

Consoled gauri with a sweet smile on her beautiful face.

"No, it's fine." I reassured her.

After talking for a while and completing our work, we both went back to our home. I think gauri is completely different from me. She is an extreme extrovert and I just like to be alone. She can talk frankly to anyone. I wish I could be confident like her...

III
BEST FRIEND

Uh! Hello?

"Wake up you stupid bitch! Do you wanna lose your job?"

From the tone of her voice, I knew who it was.

"Are you still sleeping? Wake up!"

Again, a thrilling voice came from my phone.

"Gauri, how many times I have told you to not call me and shout in the morning?"

Yes, gauri was cussing me through the phone. Since we met, we have been close friends. She has a great personality. In fact, she is like a best friend to me. It has been 2 weeks of photography. I have got used to my new job. Also, have learned many photography tricks and a lot.

I think I am getting late. Must go to the studio.

....

"Hey yamini. How is it going?" yash asks me while shaking hand with me.

"Hey chameleon! Get away!" suddenly gauri shouts out of nowhere.

"Uhh, I am done with this woman!" yash shouts while slamming the door of his room.

"Hey gauri, why do you call yash a chameleon?"

"You don't know. He acts like a great person in front of everyone, but he is secretly toxic."

Gauri gushed while taking something out of her purse.

"What is this gauri?" I asked her with some excitement!

"You just wait and watch." "This is for you yamini". Gauri announced while giving a card to me.

"What is this about?" I insisted gauri to tell me.

"Why don't you just go to your room and read? I am a little busy. There is a good news in this for you."

I went into my room. I am so nervous to read what is exactly written in this card. In addition, when I read the card.... I fell down due to terror.

It is written as,

"Dear yamini,

Due to you absolute masterpiece in photography, we request you to accept our offer. We would like to invite you to click professional photos at the concert in California of our popular superstar and singer, Andrew. We also would like you to take interview of some superstars. This chance will make you a popular and famous photographer, which is everyone's dream. Waiting for your reply.

Director

Shawn

IV
THE FEAR

"Congratulations yami..."

"Yamini?"

"Yamini! Yamini! What happened to you?"

I hear gauri mumbling to me.

"Yamini, you should have been happy and why is this precious card lying on the floor? Yamini? What happened to you?

I hear gauri stammering hundreds of words in front of me. I did not cared. I was scared. I wanted to cry. My fear had come in front of me again.

'Yamini!" are you listening to me?"

"Gauri, I need some time to be alone." I sobbed and ran to the bathroom.

I wanted to cry. I did not wanted to know anyone about my fear. It does not matter how much I try but I will never be able to forget my phobia. I have to face it. No matter how much I try.

"Yamini... are you okay?"

I hear gauri comforting me while her hand on my shoulder.

"If anything is troubling you, tell me. I will help you."

"Gauri, are you sure that what is written on that card is real?"

I gasped. I wanted to know that this was a prank or not. I hope and I wish this were not true.

"Not at all yamini. This is true. Yes, you have been given a precious chance to make you future bright and get out of this lonely and depressing life." Gauri said.

"I think that you can't believe that you have given such a chance. I understood yamini. Yes, I know that these are the tears of your happiness." Admired gauri.

"No, you misunderstood. It's not that...."

I was about to finish my sentence but then gauri stopped me.

"Oh, I know yamini. No need to explain me. I will send a reply from you to the director. I cannot wait to see you giving interviews after becoming a famous photographer.

"No gauri, stop...!"

Before I could say something, she went away.

Why can't gauri understand? Why can't she understand that I am afraid of...?

V
THE TRUTH

"So yamini, what's the feeling of becoming famous photographer?"

"Yeah, how does it feel to be the best photographer in this city?" Yamini! How does it feel? Yamini...

...

...

Aaaaaaahhhhhhhhhh! Oh! It was a dream. A nightmare. This cannot be true. I do not want to face people. I hope gauri have not replied to the director. I shall call her right now.

"Uh hello? Yamini? Why have you called me?"

"Gauri, please tell me that you haven't replied to the director from my side."

"Yes I have yamini. Do not worry; you have a precious chance. The director will be waiting for you tomorrow at the studio." Said gauri.

"Now let me sleep. Bye."

"I can't believe this! This is happening for real. I cannot face this. I do not want to be popular. I just wanted to be a simple photographer. Now what will I do?"

All the thoughts are arising in my mind. I cannot decide what I shall do.

I... I am confused. I do not want to deal with this all again. I do not want everyone to talk about me....

Next day...

(In the morning)

I do not want to go to the studio. What shall I do? Even though, if I deny the director, everyone will still talk about me. They will judge me for not accepting such a great offer. I will have to face this, no matter what I do.

With nervousness, I get in my car and drive away to meet the director.

"Good morning sir"!

"Ah, good morning yamini. I am very impressed by your photography." Said director Shawn.

"We are going to California after 3 days. Get ready. The ticket to the concert will be free for you. All the appliances will be provided to you there only."

"Sir!" I wanted to tell him that I do not want to go but I could not.

"Yamini, the rest of the details will be given to you by yash." These were the last words of the director and then he went away in his luxurious car.

"Yamini"...

I hear someone call my name.

"Uh yes?" It was yash.

"You didn't tell me about this." He said with some dissatisfaction.

"About what yash?"

"About this California thing and that you were selected for such a great opportunity."

"I forgot, sorry". I apologized and went away. I knew he was jealous. I should have listened to gauri that he was really a chameleon. The thing is that I am stressed about what is going to happen in California with me. Moreover, how will I deal with my phobia?

VI
FAINTED

Today is the day. I have to go to California for clicking pictures of the superstar, Andrew. The thing I am worried about is taking their interview. I just really cannot deal with that. Even if I deal with both of them, I do not want to be famous.

(Meanwhile, at the airport)

"Are you ready yamini?"

The director asks me.

"Yes sir", I reply with hesitation. I am scared.

....

The plane is taking off. I can see my heartbeat go faster and faster. I do not know what will happen next.

....

Finally, we reached California. We get into the hotel. I get a beautiful room but that beauty does not go against my terror. Tomorrow is the day when I will get to face my phobia. I hope and wish that everything went well.

(Next day)...

It's 5'o clock. I have to reach to the concert.

Oh, shit! Gauri has called me 100 times. She might be worried about me. I am already scared. I do not want to share this with her.

....

"I hope you are ready for becoming famous. This is the best opportunity for you. This is the first time you will experience this. Hope for doing well."

Said the director.

"And yamini, we expect you to take good interview of our superstar."

"Yes sir". I replied with fake confidence.

I entered the concert. I am scared. I want to scream. Those loud noises, everyone seeing me. I ignore the noise. I start clicking photos while the singer is singing. I tried to be focused so that my photos look professional but at the same time, I do not want to click good photos because I do not want to be known by everyone.

I am confused. However, I continue. I had clicked some great pics. The concert was over too. It was my time to take the interview. I was the first one to take an interview of a new and popular singer. I sat on a chair. My feet were trembling with fear. The famous singer is in front of me. His name is Andrew. He is handsome. He is smart and confident. Everyone is looking at me and waiting for me to ask him a question. However, whenever I try, my voice shrinks. I am not able too. I am having pain in my head. I start to remember those old and haunting memories. I cannot. I want to get out of here. I am crying inside.

I remember nothing before I fainted there.

…………

I open my eyes. It is blurry. I cannot see anything but I know that I am in someone's lap. I do not know who it is but he is gentle. I start to see something. In front of my eyes there are camera clicking my pictures. People asking me questions. No, I do not want to face it all.

I scream. I scream loudly. I hide my face in the person's chest who was holding me.

"Please! Leave me alone. I do not want any media to be here. Please take these cameras away!

I cried as loud as I could! Then I fainted again.

……………

VII
ON TELEVISION

I had slept deeply yesterday night. I do not know what to do today? I do not know how I will face the director. I fresh myself and switch on the TV but I see something horrible.

It is... it is me!

How can I be such an idiot?

I was on the TV. The news was about an interviewer fainted on the set and our famous singer Andrew helped her. This media makes a small thing into a big issue. This news was about Andrew helping me but I know that people will ask me questions. I do not want that. They may also make bad assumptions about me like... like the past!

I cannot face that. I will not get out of my room. I will stay inside the hotel until I have some money. I do not know what I will do next. I was too stressed so I ordered a cup of coffee.

....

• 22 •

"This is your coffee, ma'am!"

The waiter gave me a cup.

"Thank you". I said.

I was about to close the door until I heard her voice.

"Are you... are you the lady who is on TV in Andrew's lap?"

I was shocked. Now what shall I say? I did not responded to her question and closed the door. I must get out of California but I cannot! I was thinking all of this until I hear a ring on the door.

"Yamini, open the door. We have to go back."

It was the director. He was angry and of course, he should be. How can I convince him that I do not want to go?

"We will miss the flight. You have already embarrassed us a lot."

I was pinched by this sentence. I really had insulted them but how could I control my fear?

"Are you coming or not?"

I hear a frustrated voice again.

"Sir, I have booked my flight. I will go alone."

I lied. I had no choice. I could not have gone with the team.

"Fine then."

After saying this, he left. He did not even asked me if I was okay. I cannot believe what I have done!

Now I do not know what to do. I can just sit silent.

Gauri! Yes, I can call her, but... I do not want to.

VIII
SURPRISE

It has been 3 days since I have been in this room. Gauri has called me multiple times but I did not picked up her call. I am afraid. I do not know what, but I am.

....

"I can't stay here forever." I think to myself.

Whenever I close my eyes, my past comes in front of me. I do not know how I can deal with it. I just want to leave this world, this toxic media! These toxic people. While I was reasoning my thoughts, I get a call from gauri. This is the hundredth time she is calling me. Such a bad friend I am.

"Why aren't you picking up the call?" I perceive a sexy voice from the back. I turn around to see and I do not believe my eyes.

It.... It was Andrew. How can him...

"What are you doing here?"

I yell in surprise while he was coming closer to me. He was not replying to my question.

"How did you come here and why are you here?"

He was a well-known VIP. Why would he search for me? An average girl.

"Why are you...?"

I was about to throw another interrogation but he pushed me towards the wall and blocked me from running away.

"No more questions. I want to ask you something."

"But why?" I was about to roar while he covered my mouth with his manly hands.

"Just reply to my questions."

He interrogated me. I tried repeatedly to run and talk back but I could not. He was too strong and of course a celebrity. Therefore, I too lost hope.

"Tell me, why are you afraid of success, being famous, interviews, being known to people?"

He demanded.

I was astonished. Why did he wanted to know?

"Tell me."

"I don't want to and I will not." I shouted back. I will not and have not shared to anyone about my fears. Why should I tell him?

"You will have to." He threatened me. I tried to escape but I could not. I had to tell him. I had no choice. He had the most power.

"Okay. I will tell you, but promise me you won't deduce anyone about it." I said even though I did not trusted him.

"Won't give you a chance to complain," he expressed.

I begin telling him the story of my life.

....

IX
OLD MEMORIES

My fear... my terror... it all began there when I was 14 years old. Our family did not had enough money. My parents were worried about me. Therefore, my mom started doing a job of a babysitter for me. It was a normal day. Everything was going all right until my mom... my mom... her... she died in a car accident....

I was in a trauma and so my dad too. He lived his wife. He was not able to lay hold all of this happening. First, he was worried for me; secondly, he was emotional for mom. He became weak. Everything started to fall apart. I left my school because we did not had enough money. I started doing mom's job.

One day, I came late and... and when I reached at home. I saw... I saw something unbelievable. My father was hanging. Bloo... blo... blood was tripping from his toes and neck. He had committed suicide. He left a note for me. It was written as...

"*Yamini, I love you. I am sorry I left you but I cannot live without your mom. I am going away. Yamini, there is one last wish of mine that is I failed from life, but you can't*".

I was screaming in pain. Everything had been over. My father, my mom, there was no one else in this world.

I wanted to suicide but I could not because of my father's last wish. He left easily but let me to fight on my own. Therefore, I started earning money at a shady restaurant that was enough for me. However, life was not easy for me.

People started making rumors about me. They said that I have... I have killed my father. Some said that I poisoned him. Some people even made assumptions that I killed both my parents.

Life was starting to become difficult for me. I began to have panic attacks; I was in depression in a young age. I wanted to die but I could not. I... I stopped having social interactions. Loud noises gave me attacks. People asking me questions was my biggest fear. I lived this way for 5 years until I moved to a different place and started doing photography course and this is how I ended up here.

X
CLOSE

"Yamini!" I hear a low voice in my ears. I did not noticed when I started crying. Andrew hugged me tight and was rubbing my hair with his hands.

"I... I" I was incapable of speaking.

"No need to justify. I understand." Andrew persuaded while hugging me tight. My tears were not stopping. They were flowing like an ocean. I did not realized that I wetted his shirt with my soar tears.

"I am sorry for your shirt."

"My shirt?" he gave me an astonished look.

"Are you kidding me? You are worried about my shirt." He scolded.

"But you are a celebri..."

"Shut up!" He criticized again.

"I told you everything about me. Now what do you want from me and why the hell are you asking me all this." I asked.

"You'll know soon".

"By the way, I came in your room through your window." He laughed and went out of the room while covering his face with a mask.

"Was I dreaming? What the fuck just happened?"

A famous person just came in my room and got to know each and everything about me.

While I was trying to understand my messed up life.

Gauri called me again.

"Hello!"

"Yamini, are you okay? Why didn't you fucking picked up my call?"

"I... I"

"Yamini, where are you? In addition, why haven't you come back? What's happening there?"

I was not in a state to answer her questions. I ended the call and blocked her.

......

XI

COFFEE

It has been many days since I have been staying in this hotel. I am running out of money. I wonder how I will manage in the upcoming days. People might have forgot about that fainting incident. So maybe, I can go outside.

I went to a coffee shop without wasting any much of time. I have been feeling very ill inside the hotel room.

.....

"One dalgano coffee please".

I ordered and then sat alone next to a window. Everything is so hard in my life. Why can't I live like a normal person? Why only I have to face all this.

"Your order ma'am".

I am knocked out of my thoughts.

"Hmm... thank you!"

It has been many days since I drank my favorite coffee.

"Excuse me, can I sit here?"

A smart looking person asks me. I cannot see his face. He was wearing a black hoodie. I wanted to be alone but still I agreed.

"Yes, you can!"

He had a nice, masculine body. He looked like someone I had met before but I didn't know like whom?

"So you like dalgano coffee too".

He asked me while taking out his wallet.

"Umm, yes I guess."

I did not know what to say. His voice was familiar.

"What's your name?" He asked me.

"Yamini". I said.

"Here is your bill ma'am". The waiter interrupts. Before I was about to pay the person took out his money and gave.

"Here take it".

"Thank you sir", the waiter went away.

What just happened? Why did he pay for me? He does not even know me.

"Why did you pay for me?" I interrogated.

"You might have less money so I thought of paying."

How did he know that I have less money? I was shocked.

"Who are you?" I asked.

"Andrew".

"Wha...." I was about to shout but then he covered my mouth.

"Don't shout". "I want to talk to you". He said.

"About what?" I persuaded.

"Just come with me". He held my hand and took me towards a car. It was Bugatti Chiron, which is worthing 2.9 million. It was my favorite car too.

"Get in". He whispered.

"In thi... this car!"

Was I dreaming? I could not imagine riding in this car.

"Yes". He said with a smile on his face. His smile was adorable. I got in the car. It was comfortable as hell. I could not imagine what I was seeing. I was in a Bugatti with a famous singer. It was as if I had forgot all my stress for a second.

Andrew tied my seat belt. He was sure handsome and breathtaking.

"Where are you taking me?" I gushed.

"To a place you'll love". He declared.

"Please say that we will be alone there."

I continued in terror.

"Don't worry". He whispered again.

XII
STAY WITH ME

"Here we are". Andrew stopped.

I looked out of the window. It was beautiful. It was a river flowing, making heartwarming noises. The scenery, it was enthralling. Cold winds were blowing magnificently. I could hear the charming sound of nature. It was captivating.

"Do you like it?"

Andrew asked.

"Lovely". I could not control my tears. I was away from the world, alone. I wish I could live here forever.

"You have to come and stay with me". Andrew resumed.

"With you?" that was not possible. There were many reasons for me to not stay with him.

"Yes. If you will not live with me then where are you going to go? You don't have any money nor do you have a house here."

"How did you know that I don't have any money? How do you know so much about me?" I commanded.

"I have known a lot about you since the day I met you."

"Why are you helping me?" I asked.

"You will know soon". "Now tell me. Will you come with me?"

He asked.

"I can't... I... do not want to be recognized by people. I do not want to be known by anyone. Also, I don't know how I will pay you back."

"Don't worry about paying me back and about people, you won't be known by anyone." He said.

I had no choice. It was the only way I could choose. So I agreed with him.

XIII
YOUR HOME

"Here we are to your apartment". Andrew said.

"I...I don't know how to thank you."

"You need not". He repeated. I hugged him. No matter how famous he was but he was the only one who took care of me here.

"Goodnight". I said.

"Goodnight to you too and don't worry too much." He replied.

I entered my apartment. It was wholesome. Andrew had known everything about my interests. It was like my dream house. I refreshed myself and went to sleep. On the bed, there was a note written that,

"Be ready tomorrow. I would like to take you somewhere."

Andrew

Where would he like to take me? I just wish that no drama happened tomorrow.

....

I try to sleep but I cannot. I am excited about tomorrow.

....

.....

I had a great sleep last night. I wish everything were like this for lifetime.

I need to get ready fast...

After a long period, I had felt some happiness in my heart. I was not worried now. Everything was all right.

I get dressed and wait for Andrew to pick me up. I have many questions for him. I see a car arriving.

"Hey, so I think I am late huh?" Andrew apologized.

"No, you are right on time." I persisted.

"So, shall we go?"

"Yaa, sure." I said and got into the car.

"Andrew, how do you get so much time? And why do people don't recognize you?"

"I just get some time, I don't know how." He answered.

It was strange.

How can he get away with so much time?

"So, where are you going to take me?" I asked.

"You'll get to know shortly." He gushed.

XIV
A NEW JOB

"Here we are". Andrew declared while stopping his car next to a large building.

"What is this place?" I asked. This place looks like a royal and luxurious office.

"This is the place where you will work."

"I...I will work!" I did not understand what Andrew was trying to say.

"Yes. This is your new job."

"My... my new job?" I shouted.

"Yes, is there a problem?" he doubted.

"No. there… there is… not a problem but…" I was uncertain.

"Would you like to go back to your place to face your boss and others who left you alone in an unknown country?" Andrew hissed in anger.

"No… I… did not meant that…

Before I could say something, he interrupted in anger.

"Then what do you mean?"

"Listen… Andrew, do not be angry please. I am just nervous and a bit unsure about how fast everything is happening and you are such a big personality that…

"Stop saying I am a big personality. If I am famous then it does not means that I cannot talk with anyone. Can't I just have a normal close friend like you?"

"You really don't think of me as a small person. You consider me as your friend."

I gasped in shock. I really believed that he considered me as an emotional ready.

"Not just a friend but a close one," he said and looked into my eyes. His gentle eyes were like a small world in which I would love to live in. he was about to say something more *when an employee breaked in.*

"Good morning sir! Sir you should have informed us. We would have sent a driver for you." The employee said in stress.

"No thanks". Andrew sent the employee back and then looked towards me.

"So yamini, are you coming with me? I give you two choices. Whether you go back to your old place and face your fear again or stay here, do a job, earn and live."

It was an easy thing also a difficult option to pick at the same time. There are many things. If I stay here, in California, I will have to think about many things. About my future, my belongings but it is even worse if I go back to my place. I will have to face everyone and I do not want that.

Therefore, I choose to do the job, which Andrew was offering, to me and stay permanently here.

"I think I will settle here without facing anything." I say to Andrew.

"That's a great choice". He replied.

XV

A NEW START OF LIFE

"Would you not like to see your new office?"

He said.

"Of course, why not?" I answered with enthusiasm.

Andrew showed me his large and luxury office. It was a photography studio but it was excessively large and beautiful. It was mind-blowing. Its stunning and hallucinating look just made me feel in love with it.

"So, here is our new workaholic. Her name is Yamini. I expect all of you to treat her nicely."

Andrew ordered to his employees. On the other hand, I was feeling uncomfortable and in pain. Everyone was looking at me. Cannot I work in a place where there is just very less employees or me.

"Andrew, I am feeling uncomfortable. Everyone is staring at me."

I whispered to him.

"Don't worry. No one will talk to you here. Everyone is busy in their own work".

He gave me a relief.

"Now I expect all of you to go back to your work without any further communications."

He ordered once more.

Despite that, I was exploring the whole studio which I thought was an office."

"Andrew, is this your own studio? Don't you have any boss on your head?"

"Um, I do have a lot of bosses but I am not scared of them and yeah this is my own studio."

He replied.

"It's astonishing".

"You like that?" He asked.

"Well of course. Who wouldn't like a great place like this?"

"Then you would love the place, where I am going to take you tomorrow." Said Andrew with a huge, wide smile on his face.

I hated this habit of Andrew. Firstly, he would put me in suspense and then he would never answer to any of my questions.

"Why do you always have to put me in suspense? I HATE YOU!"

I hissed.

"I love teasing you." He laughed making me even angrier.

"Okay. I will have to go. You can explore this place for the time." He calmed me down.

"Okay, bye."

"Bye". He went away.

I had a lot of leisure time. This was the first time I was free from work and stress. I explored the studio. The cleanliness here was outstanding. The paintings, the photos were just amazing. I could also see the beautiful nature from the studio. There were many plants whose aroma just made my mind relief. The flowers, the trees, grass, the birds, the sounds, I could just dive into this deep world of nature. I wish everything remained like this. I wish nothing ever changes. I close my eyes, listen and smell to the graceful sounds along with the fresh fragrance of flowers, which gives peace to my heart.

XVI
DO HE LIKES YOU?

"Oh my fuck! This all shit happened to you in just these few days."

Gauri gasped in shock.

"Yes gauri. If Andrew wasn't here then I would have literally died."

I told gauri everything except about my fear.

"Umm, yamini. Can I ask you a question?"

"Yeah sure". I replied.

"I think. Tha... that. Umm... he... he has a crush on you". Gauri said while hesitating.

"What? No! Never. It can't happen."

I shouted in anger.

"Why are you overreacting yamini?"

Uhh, how can I tell gauri that if this thought of hers comes true then I would have to face people. Andrew is a famous singer and if his fans come to know that he has a crush on me then I would die due to the thought of facing everyone. I would be on TV, in people's mind and everyone would be staring at me and...

"Yamini! Yamini! Are you lost in your dreams again?"

"Uhh, sorry gauri. I will call you later. Bye". I ended the call.

I just wish and hope that Andrew does not like me. However, what if he really does. What will I do then? No... no... no... I... I am just overthinking. This cannot happen. Never! Now everything is settled. Andrew would never let me face my phobia again. Yes, I know it. While I was drowning in the deep ocean of my thoughts, I received a message from Andrew.

ANDREW

"Are you sleeping?"

YAMINI

No. why?

ANDREW

"I was just thinking if you could come with me tomorrow...

(Typing)...

....

What is he typing? He would like me to come with him tomorrow but where?

....

ANDREW

And meet me at the park.

………………………..

OH, he scared me. I thought he would ask me to meet me somewhere in a crowded place.

…………………….

YAMINI

"Sure I would."

ANDREW

"Love to"

Okay. Will meet you at Destiny garden.

Goodnight Yamini (Heart emoji).

XVII
WAS GAURI CORRECT?

OH. Why does he want to meet me at the park? Wait... let me reply to him or I will seem rude.

....

ANDREW

"Are you sleeping?"

YAMINI

"No, why?"

ANDREW

I was just thinking if you could come with me tomorrow...

And meet me at the park?

YAMINI

"Sure, I would".

ANDREW

"Love to".

Okay. Will meet you at Destiny garden.

Good night yamini (Heart emoji).

YAMINI

"Goodnight to you too."

ANDREW

(Smile emoji)

……………..

And… sent.

But… but wait a minute. He… he sent me a heart emoji. Oh my god! No one is my whole life has talked to me as casually. What does a heart emoji mean? Do he really likes me? No. no… I am overthinking. It is all because of this gauri.

Afterwards, I washed my face and fell asleep.

……………..

RingRing**Ring**

Uhhh. Not this alarm again.

I hate waking up! But I have to meet Andrew today.

I get dressed in my tomboy clothes. I was never worried about my clothing or my face, as I never wished to attract people towards myself. This is just one benefit of my fear. Still... it is far worse.

I reach to destiny garden using a cab. It may be astonishing to hear but people rarely come in this garden. Once Andrew told me that, it is because there is a rumor that ghosts live here. However, I do not... believe in ghosts. I think to myself.

I walk out of the cab and only one thought come to my mind after seeing my surroundings.

Ghost! Really?

How can people believe that ghosts live here? This place is heaven!

"Am I late?"

I hear someone's voice from the back.

"Not at all. You are right on time."

I smiled towards him.

"So…"

Andrew tried to break the silence but I am too introverted for him.

"Well, you are not too girly if I observe you".

Andrew said.

"Umm. Well… the thing is that I like being comfortable."

How can I tell him that I do not want to attract people…?

"Anyways, you look beautiful in anything you wear." He said with a huge wide smile on his face.

XVIII

HE COMPLIMENTED ME

What the heck? He complimented me. Does he really think I am beautiful? Was gauri correct? No. no. calm down yamini. Reply to him.

"Thank you". I said.

"No problem. Well, be ready. We will go on a vacation after one week."

"Vacation? But I haven't worked for so many days."

I asked.

"Who said the vacation is for you? It's for me and you are coming with me to click pictures."

He said.

"OH. I misunderstood."

I apologized.

"If you really want some more time to relax then it's okay."

He tried to comfort me.

"No. No its fine! I want to work hard!" I said with enthusiasm.

"Just make sure there are not many people there."

"Won't give you a chance to complain." He calmed me.

……………………

Hmm... Andrew and I talked a lot today. I have to know about their interests and his work but he never told me about his family. I asked a lot but he changed the topic in every single way he could. I also, then left the hope. We went to eat ice cream together and I must say that he really cares about me. He has a great personality.

Wait... wait a minute...

"WHY THE HECK AM I THINKING SO MUCH ABOUT HIM?"

No no no yamini. Focus on your work. May be... I can call gauri but she will make me overthink again. No. I must work. I cannot sleep too.

I do not remember. While working when I fell asleep on the table.

....

Aww. Ouch! My neck hurts! It's 9'o clock. I must have slept on bed. Now I feel tired but I need to work. With all these thoughts raising in my mind, I proceed to the studio.

....

(At the studio)

*Hmm... no one is talking to me. **OH**, this feels so good. Now I can work peacefully. I need to edit some pics too.*

....

It has been some hours since I am working. May be I should rest.

Ring*

I received an SMS

BANK

Dear customer,

$ 42,770 has been transferred to your bank account.

....

What…! Who transferred this much money in my account?

Ring Ring*Ring Ring

Andrew is calling me.

"Hello? Andrew?"

"Yamini, have you received your salary in your account?"

Oh. So this was my salary. I must say, I am going to be rich soon if I continue getting this amount of money.

"Yamini?"

Andrew interrupted.

"Umm, yes yes. I have it. Thanks to you Andrew."

I thanked.

"You deserve this for your work."

He replied.

XIX
VACATION

It has been 1 week since I have been working I have some experience too. Today I have to go with Andrew. He said we would be going to a waterfall location. I do not know. I just wish that I did not mess things up there.

Okay. I have to reach to the studio.

……………. ……………. …………… …………

(At the studio)

"Ready to go?"

I hear someone (Andrew) whispering in my ear.

"Yeah!"

I said with enthusiasm.

"There will be no one else going with us right?"

I asked in a worried tone.

"Don't worry. Just a few people."

Ahhh. Thank god. I cannot wait to go to that location. I just love nature. The sounds of it. It is just... so enthralling.

"Shall we go? Get in the car."

He asked.

"Yeah yeah. Just a second."

I sat down in the car.

Hmm... wait... wait. Will I go alone with him? I thought we would have separate cars. Will he drive himself? Shall I ask him? But that may seem rude but what will be his reply? Moreover,

"Hey! What is my little yamini thinking about?"

He said while rubbing my head.

"I... lit... little yamini?"

I froze. Firstly his hand was on my head and secondly he called me little yamini and like... so casually with a straight face?

"Yes. Can't I call you that?"

"Umm. Yes you can!"

I replied. I did not wanted to seem rude.

The whole ride was quite. I am quite introverted and Andrew is not a lot talkative too. I just felt like peace. I was feeling the cold, swinging winds touching my face. I was just enjoying as heaven. I plugged my earphones in my ears and listened to some of my favorite songs. I had always liked sad songs, and I must say... my half playlist is filled with Andrew's album. His voice is just so calming.

"So you like my voice huh?" Andrew talked while peeking into my phone.

"Um... yeah. I mean. It's not like..."

"Okay, don't panic." He said while covering my mouth.

I was a little embarrassed. And yeah, it was the third time he has covered my mouth.

"Why do you like covering my mouth so much?" I asked in embarrassment to change the topic.

"So that I can feel your lips." He said.

What did he said? Is he...?

"I am just kidding, now don't overthink again." He laughed.

Oh, thank god. If a statement of his were true then I would have literally jumped out of the car due to my fear.

XX

SAVED FROM DROWNING

"So here we are". Andrew said while stopping the car.

Wow. This place is so beautiful. I mean how many times I said wow this month. Literally, my life is like heaven now.

"Do you like this place?"

He asked.

"Love it!" I replied while getting out of the car and enjoying the scenery. When I turned back, I saw Andrew and he had covered his face.

"Why have you cove...?"

"So that these tourists can't recognize me." He answered in between.

"Let's go." He said.

"Yes".

I know how it would be feeling to wear a mask everywhere to not be recognized from people. I have suffered from this too... when... people... throwed fake allegations on me. I had... to cover my face in shame even though it was... not my... fault.

I was about to cry while thinking of all this when Andrew took my hand and handed me my camera.

"What are you waiting about? Now come, show me your skills." He claimed.

I took back my tears. I did not wanted him to worry about me.

"Yeah, sure." I replied with a smile on my face.

....

I had clicked a lot pictures and I must say that I am proud of myself. May be I should click one more picture. Yeah, of that flower.

Ahh... this lens is too big. If I go a little back then maybe a good photograph will come. Just a little more back. And just...

"Yamini... wait...!"

I hear Andrew screaming and running towards me.

"Why is he so worri...?

OH no..."

"Ahh..."

I remember nothing until I was drowning. I could not breathe properly. I do not know how to swim. Someone help! I tried to scream but I could not...

I remember nothing until I fainted.

• 73 •

………….. ……………… …………. ………….

It is blurry.

Ahh… someone is holding me. Are people clicking my photos? Is this scene repeating itself? ahh… my body hurts!

XXI
IN HOSPITAL

"Ahh... Where am I? Where is Andrew?" I was in hospital. No one else was there. My head is hurting. What happened these past few hours? Where is everyone? Where is my phone?

Oh. Here it is. I shall call Andrew.

The person you are calling is busy. Please try again later

What? What shall I do now?

"Ma'am, are you okay?" I hear a nurse saying.

"Where... is..." umm wait. I should not ask where Andrew is to her or something horrible can happen.

"Never mind. Can you pass me a glass of water?" I asked gently.

"Yes ma'am, sure." The nurse went away.

I observed the room. I... I am in VIP room. But how can that happen?

"Ma'am water".

"Oh. Thanks."

"Ma'am, Sir Andrew was very worried about you. He even sat down beside you for a long time until he had some urgent work."

"Pffffffttttt". I split out water from my mouth out of shock. How does she know that Andrew was with me?

"How do you know that I was with Andrew?"

"Ma'am not just me but the whole city knows." The nurse said smiling.

What! What the fuck. How can it be possible? Wait. What on earth!

I checked my phone and I got this...

HOLLYWOOD NEWS

Today headlines

"Rock star Andrew's girlfriend saved from drowning at the waterfall location. Both couples founded in worry.

Comments: -

Nicole: - Aww... they look so cute together. But I do not think this woman is too suitable for our handsome Andrew.

Peter: - Just look at her! I have to know about her and she is that girl who fainted on the interview before. She is also a professional photographer.

....

• 77 •

No no no! Now everyone has to know about me! And this news is fake. I am not his girlfriend.

And... and when did he kissed me? There was a photo in this website of him kissing me! I was unconscious at that time. No. no. I want to die. I want to...

I had panic attack again and I fainted.

XXII

I LOVE YOU

"Yamini? Wake up".

I hear someone whispering in my ear.

I was at my home. In my room.

"Andrew, you are here. Help me. What is all this mess? This website and these photos. This is not true, right. Tell me? This is a Photoshop and this is a prank! Please tell me. I don't want to face all this."

"I am sorry yamini. But... this is true. Yes, I kissed you. But it was to save your life. I couldn't do anything else." He expressed in sorrow.

"What do you mean you kissed me to save me? You could have let me die peacefully. What is this for? At least dying

was better than to face all this. What am I going to do now? Have you read the comments? What people are thinking about me?"

I cried and pushed him away. I wanted to die. I do not want to live.

"Yamini, listen to me. Dying is not the solution of...

"No, you listen to me. You do not know how it feels like to repeat the old, hurtful past. I cannot face all this. You may be able to but I cannot... I..."

"Stop yamini!"

He shouted and kissed me. How could he dare...?

His breathe was warm but I wanted to push him away. He was too strong. I was crying. My tears were not stopping. The past was repeating itself.

"Listen to me yamini. I do not give a fuck of these websites. I just want to say that I... I LOVE YOU".

What? Gauri was correct. He... he

"Yamini, you need to be strong. You have to face all this. It is true I have a crush on you. I love you and nothing is fake in this website. I have already considered you as my girlfriend in front of media.

"What... Andrew... I thought... you... you would at least understand... my pain. But... I HATE YOU. Go away."

I pushed him out of my room. I cried as loudly as I could. Mom! Dad! I need you. I cannot face this world all alone.

I want to die!

XXIII

LIFE HAS BECOME DARK

I did not slept last night. I was worried, anxious, panicked and stressed at the same time. I cannot go outside. The media will be waiting for me.

Wait. 44 missed calls from Andrew. I am not picking up his call. It is all because of him. I hate him. I could have died peacefully but no. now what will I do? It was not this silly to drown in water.

But if I remember, what he said yesterday.

"Listen to me yamini. I do not give a fuck of these websites. I just want to say that I... I love you".

....

I... just cannot really help. But is it really his fault? Do I also love him? Even though if I had loved him then my love would not go against my terror.

What shall I do now?

Shall I call him?

Knock* Knock

Someone is on my door.

"Yamini, it's me Andrew. Please open the door. I... I am sorry".

I really want to open the door but my fear is not letting me to.

"Andrew please, leave me alone." I cried.

"But yamini..."

"Just go away." I shouted.

"Okay. I am sorry yamini. I hope you will be okay."

"I am fine!" I lied.

....

My life... it is dark again. No joy. No happiness. Just my terror and fear. I wonder... if Andrew was correct. Will I have to face my fear no matter what? Is this the only way to be happy in life?

I just do not want to live. Dad... why have you left me in such a situation? I hate everyone. Everyone is selfish!

I just want to sleep.

..

"Yamini, you will have to face your fear. No matter what."

"Yes yamini. It's not that hard as you think."

"Yamini, don't be like you father. Fight for your life."

"But dad..."

Ahh... a dream.

Dad, Mom!

I started crying again. Why can't I just live like a normal person? I do not know what to do next. I will. I will stay at home until I feel like going out.

XXIV
FACE IT

It has been one week since I am at home. I have not talked to Andrew. He come to my home daily but I never opened the door. He called me a multiple times but I never replied. I know... that he do not deserve this but I cannot help.

Today... I have thoughts to go to the studio and face everything... and if... I would not be able to... then may be... I will suicide...

...

I booked a cab.

Take me to the...

"Ma'am, why are you in a taxi? You are yamini, a professional photographer and Andrew's girlfriend, right. You should have a Ferrari or something."

Before I was about to say something the driver interrupted.

I got out of the car immediately. I did not wanted to tell him the whole story or even face him. I had rented a small car, so maybe I can go in it.

I entered the studio and what I saw was horrible.

Media, cameras, interviewers, people...

One of the reporter saw me and came running towards me. He started asking questions.

"Here, Andrew's girlfriend, yamini. So where were you from these past few days?"

Another reporter then came towards me.

"Yes ma'am. We need answers."

They all started asking questions. I started having pain in my head. And the next thing I saw was that Andrew was just looking at me. He was not helping me. Why was he acting like this?

I just went away to my home. I did not wanted to face this media again.

………………..

I reached at home. No. I cannot face. I would die if I live like this. Interviews, people, famous...

I just... cannot... I do not want to... only one thing is left to do now...

<u>SUICIDE</u>

XXV
SUICIDE

I don't think I will be able to do anything more in life and Andrew... why was he just standing and looking? Why wasn't he helping me? What is wrong with him?

I do not want media to gossip about me after my death. I am writing a suicide note.

....

I am done with my life...

I am depressed, anxious and stressed with the way my life is. My fear, my terror will not let me live happily. I tried my best but I could not face it. All I did was run away from the situation that made me uncomfortable instead of facing them.

I am sorry...

Yamini

....

I think this is enough for media to understand why I left my life and killed myself.

I am sorry mom, dad. I could not reach up to your expectations. Sorry dad, I could not complete your last wish. I always wanted to be strong but I could not. I am a failure. I know that...

I am coming to you. Mom and dad. My last tear dropped from my eye and...

"Yamini. STOP!"

"Andrew, leave me alone!"

"I said stop yamini!"

Andrew came in running. He broke the door. He lifted me up in his arms in hurry.

"What the fuck do you think you are doing?"

He shouted while looking at my face in anger.

"I want to die. I cannot face. I cannot fight. I am not strong."

I cried.

He made me sit on the bed and cleaned up all the mess. He read the suicide note and tore it up into pieces.

"I didn't expected you to be this weak." He said while tearing the paper.

"But Andrew..."

"What do you mean by this? Do you think killing yourself will solve all your problems? No. suicide just passes your problems to another person. It never helps in making your life peaceful. He shouted.

"Do you even know how I would live if I had lost you. If I was just a second late then you might have left this world." He was roaring aloud. I never saw him like this. Emotional, angry, stressed.

"But Andrew... you don't know how it feels to have this fear..."

"Yamini! I know the most about how this feels." He said.

"I lost someone precious to me just because of this so called fucking Scopophobia and this terror of facing people."

"Som... someone precious". I was astonished.

"You always wanted to know about my family right? I'll tell you today".

He said.

XXVI
HIS PAST

"It was my sister".

"Your sister".

I asked.

"Yes. She had the same fear you have. The difference is just a fear of hers was from birth. She did not suffered from any trauma like you sis. So her fear was difficult to cure." He cried.

"Andrew".

I tried to comfort him.

"I always thought... that... that this was not a big deal but I never knew how much she was suffering from it."

"My dream was to become famous but I never knew that because... of me... she... would take such a... large step." Tears started coming out of Andrew's eyes.

"Andrew... I... I am sorry."

"Then one day, when I told her that my dream was to... become famous and she smiled at me and said that I will surely become famous. I just failed to understand that her smile was fa... fake."

"And one day... I was... her suicide note... like you had written... she said... that... she was a... interruption for... my... dream... to achieve..."

I felt like someone had crushed my heart into pieces. I felt like it was me... who was responsible for her death."

"Andrew... it was not your fault."

"Maybe... if I would have cared for her or... would have taken her to a psychologist. If I would have treated her medically then... may be she would have been alive."

"I... I am sorry Andrew for your loss." I never saw him crying before.

"And I want to tell you something yamini."

He said.

"This was my plan."

"What plan?"

I asked.

XXVII
HIS PLAN

"Yes, my plan. Do you remember you always asked me, why do I care for you so much?"

"Yes I remember, but it was because you had a crush on me?"

I asked hesitatingly.

"No yamini. It was something else."

He claimed.

"Let me tell you".

"The day when I met you I had some weird feeling. When you fainted...

You made me remember of my sister. Therefore, that is the reason I asked you what you afraid of are.

When I have to know that, you had the same fear that my sister had. Then I promised to myself that I would not let you lose your life because of this terror. That is the reason I asked everything about you. I wanted to make you strong not weak. I did not wanted any other person to lose their life. I wanted to confess my mistake by making you stronger and making you face your fear.

You might be wondering why didn't I helped you today. It was because I wanted you to face everything yourself without my help. But I didn't expected you to be this weak and suicide."

"No Andrew. Do not say I am weak. I am going to fight. I am going to face every situation. Now, that I have to know everything. I will never lose hope for my life."

I shouted while hugging him.

"And yeah. This girlfriend and this love thing was also a part of my plan."

He said.

"Soo... you don't love me?"

I asked.

"Who knows? Maybe?"

He looked into my eyes.

"Okay now. But what are you going to do next?"

He questioned.

"Face people."

I said with fire in my eyes.

"Yamini, I know that you are not courageous and motivated to fight. But I must tell you, to remove this fear completely... you must get a physiotherapy."

He exclaimed.

"Andrew... I had also thought of getting a therapy before but I was afraid back then. But because of you now I feel motivated. Thank you Andrew."

"Uh. Huh, do not thank to me. Thank yourself for having the courage to fight."

He motivated me once more.

"So... the media is outside... wanna face it? Are you ready?"

He professed.

"Yes, I am."

I roared.

XXVIII
FIGHT

"Okay, I'll go outside. I am sure. I will fight."

I went outside with Andrew. Everyone was their asking us questions. It was not as easy as I thought. My head started spinning again. However, I did not wanted to run away. I wanted to clear things up.

"Yamini, what's happening between you two."

"Yes. The media wants to know."

"Yamini"

"Yamini"

………………………………………………

Okay yamini… calm down.

"Quiet! It is important that media needs to know everything?

Andrew and me are just best friends. There is nothing between us and even if there is something. You all have no right to know!"

Uff. I shouted a lot. Now what will they think about me. No I shouldn't worry about people… oh no. I am fainting again.

……………………………………

Ahh. I am awake. I had fainted again. Andrew was sitting beside me.

"Andrew?"

He must be sleeping. Shall I wake him up?

"Andrew?"

"Uh yes, yamini? You are awake.

"Yes".

I replied.

"So. You fought well against your terror. Now you just need a physiotherapy and a little bit of practice to face people and I am sure you will do it."

He said trying to motivate me.

"I am sure too."

XXIX
NGO

1 year later,

It has been 1 year since that incident. I have physiotherapy and a lot has changed since then.

Along with photography, I have opened my own NGO, where I help people suffering from the same fear as I had.

I must say thanks to that person who helped me through this...

My mom and dad came a lot in my dreams. I dreamed my dad last night; he was appreciating me for my work.

I have become famous now. I have an interview in the evening today too. I have also written a book in which I have mentioned him...

• 103 •

Knock* Knock

"Come in..."

"Ma'am, someone's here to meet you."

"Who?"

I asked.

"Ma'am, he told me not to tell you his name."

"Okay. I am coming."

I wonder who that person is.

....

"Ma'am, here he is".

The servant said and went away.

"Hey!"

"Andrew..."

I shouted in joy and hugged him hard.

"You look beautiful."

He complimented.

"You too."

I said.

"I look beautiful?"

He gasped.

"No... No. I mean handsome!"

I laughed.

"So... I am happy to see you this way. Away from all your fears and joyful."

"Me too Andrew".

I jumped in joy.

"So, I heard you have an interview this evening?"

He asked.

"Umm yeah. You are correct."

I said.

"So, you are becoming more famous than me, huh?"

"Stop teasing me Andrew! Your songs. They are famous as hell."

I chuckled.

"I'll meet you at the interview yamini. Have to go. Bye."

"So early?"

I questioned.

"Nah. I'll just come back in a second."

"Bye."

I responded.

XXX

THE INTERVIEW - THAT CHANGED MY LIFE

At the interview,

"Welcome to this show. Today we have our famous photographer and the owner of scopophobia NGO, Yamini."

"Good evening".

I said.

"Good evening yamini".

The reporter said.

I observed the whole place but I do not find Andrew anywhere. Oh, he is there on the special VIP seat.

"And with yamini, we have a special person here; our famous rock star Andrew."

Claps* Claps

"So yamini, be ready. We are going to ask you a lot of questions here."

The reporter laughed."

"Yeah. I am ready."

I responded while keeping half of my eye on Andrew. He surely has grown more handsome.

....

After some time,

"So yamini, we have asked you a lot of questions. But just one last question."

The reporter asked.

"Yeah, yeah sure."

I said.

"So, in one sentence, what would you describe about your change in life?"

I knew what I had to say.

"If I would have not fainted at the interview. Then maybe... I wouldn't have been here today."

I say looking into Andrew's eyes,

●

<u>*"It was an interview that changed my life..."*</u>

I say looking into Andrew's eyes,

**<u>*"It was an interview that changed my life..."*</u>

A Message From Author

HELLO, EVERYONE HERE.

I HOPE YOU ALL ENJOYED THE STORY.

I KNOW IT WAS SHORT BUT WORTH READING.

I JUST WANT TO GIVE A MESSAGE THAT WHENEVER YOU ARE FACING ANY PROBLEM OR SITUATION IN LIFE, JUST DO NOT RUN AWAY FROM IT. FIGHT IT AND TRUST ME. IT WILL BE FINE.

EVERYTHING IS TEMPERORY ON EARTH NOTHING IS PERMANENT.

SO ENJOY THE GOOD MOMENTS AND LET NOT THE BAD MOMENTS SNATCH YOUR HAPPINESS AWAY.

LOVE YOU ALL.